Zoo Animals

Ostrich

Patricia Whitehouse

Heinemann Library
Chicago, Illinois

Customer Service 888-454-2279
Visit our website at www.heinemannlibrary.com

Designed by Sue Emerson, Heinemann Library
Printed and bound in the United States by Lake Book Manufacturing, Inc.

07 06 05 04 03
10 9 8 7 6 5 4 3 2 1

Library of Congress Cataloging-in-Publication Data
Whitehouse, Patricia, 1958-
    Ostrich / Patricia Whitehouse.
        p. cm. — (Zoo animals)
Includes index.
Summary: An introduction to ostriches, including their size, diet, and everyday behavior and highlighting differences between those in the wild and those living in zoos.
    ISBN: 1-58810-887-2 (HC), 1-40340-543-3 (Pbk.)
    1. . Ostriches—Juvenile literature. [1. Ostriches. 2. Zoo animals.] I. Title.
    QL696.S9 W48 2002
    599.63'5—dc21

                        2001008041

Acknowledgments
The author and publishers are grateful to the following for permission to reproduce copyright material:
Title page, pp. 4, 22, 24 Morton Beebe/Corbis; pp. 5, 21 D. Demello/Wildlife Conservation Society; p. 6 Richard Bickel/Corbis; p. 7 Ken Lucas/Visuals Unlimited; p. 8 Fred Bruemmer/DRK Photo; p. 9 Joe McDonald/Visuals Unlimited; p. 10L Jeremy Woodhouse/DRK Photo; p. 10R Steve Kaufman/Corbis; p. 11 Jo Prater/Visuals Unlimited; p. 12 Fran Coleman/Animals Animals; p. 13 Diane Shapiro/Wildlife Conservation Society; pp. 14, 18 Anup Shah/DRK Photo; p. 15 Brian Rogers/Visuals Unlimited; p. 16 John D. Cunningham/Visuals Unlimited; p. 17 Inga Spence/Visuals Unlimited; p. 19 M. P. Kahl/DRK Photo; p. 20 Mitsuaki Iwago/Minden Pictures; p. 23 (col. 1, T-B) Joe McDonald/Visuals Unlimited, Steve Kaufman/Corbis, Chicago Zoological Society/The Brookfield Zoo; p. 23 (col. 2, T-B) Morton Beebe/Corbis, Jim Schulz/ Chicago Zoological Society/The Brookfield Zoo, David Samuel Robbins/Corbis; back cover (L-R) Joe McDonald/Visuals Unlimited, D. Demello/Wildlife Conservation Society

Cover photograph by Ken Lucas/Visuals Unlimited
Photo research by Bill Broyles

Every effort has been made to contact copyright holders of any material reproduced in this book. Any omissions will be rectified in subsequent printings if notice is given to the publisher.

Special thanks to our advisory panel for their help in the preparation of this book:

Eileen Day, Preschool Teacher
Chicago, IL

Ellen Dolmetsch,
Library Media Specialist
Wilmington, DE

Kathleen Gilbert,
Teacher
Round Rock, TX

Sandra Gilbert,
Library Media Specialist
Houston, TX

Angela Leeper,
Educational Consultant
North Carolina Department
of Public Instruction
Raleigh, NC

Pam McDonald, Reading Teacher
Winter Springs, FL

Melinda Murphy,
Library Media Specialist
Houston, TX

We would also like to thank Lee Haines, Assistant Director of Marketing and Public Relations at the Brookfield Zoo in Brookfield, Illinois, for his review of this book.

Some words are shown in bold, **like this.**
You can find them in the picture glossary on page 23.

Contents

What Are Ostriches?

feathers

Ostriches are birds.

They have **feathers** and lay eggs.

In the wild, ostriches only live where it is warm.

But you can see ostriches at the zoo.

What Do Ostriches Look Like?

Ostriches are the tallest birds in the world.

They are taller than a person!

male

female

Male ostriches have black and white **feathers.**

Females have grayish-brown feathers.

What Do Baby Ostriches Look Like?

Baby ostriches are called **chicks.**

They come out of big eggs.

Chicks have fluffy brown and gray **feathers**.

They look more like their parents as they grow.

Where Do Ostriches Live?

In the wild, some ostriches live in **savannas.**

Some live in **deserts.**

In some zoos, ostriches live in grassy **enclosures.**

What Do Ostriches Eat?

In the wild, ostriches eat leaves and grass.

They sometimes eat bugs.

At the zoo, ostriches eat plants and **grain.**

What Do Ostriches Do All Day?

Ostriches use their beaks to clean their **feathers.**

Sometimes they take baths in pools of water.

Ostriches spend time eating.

They sometimes lie down to rest.

How Do Ostriches Sleep?

Ostriches sleep lying down.

They rest their heads on their bodies.

Sometimes ostriches stretch out their necks while they sleep.

What Sounds Do Ostriches Make?

Females ostriches are quiet.

Male ostriches make roaring sounds.

They can also hiss.

How Are Ostriches Special?

Ostriches have wings, but they can't fly.

They are fast runners.

Ostriches lay the biggest eggs
in the world.

Their eggs are as big as a
grown-up's hand.

Quiz

Do you remember what these ostrich parts are called?

Look for the answers on page 24.

?

?

?

Picture Glossary

chick
pages 8, 9

feathers
pages 4, 7, 9, 14

desert
page 10

grain
page 13

enclosure
page 11

savanna
page 10

Note to Parents and Teachers

Reading for information is an important part of a child's literacy development. Learning begins with a question about something. Help children think of themselves as investigators and researchers by encouraging their questions about the world around them. Each chapter in this book begins with a question. Read the question together. Look at the pictures. Talk about what you think the answer might be. Then read the text to find out if your predictions were correct. Think of other questions you could ask about the topic, and discuss where you might find the answers. Assist children in using the picture glossary and the index to practice new vocabulary and research skills.

Index

Answers to quiz on page 22

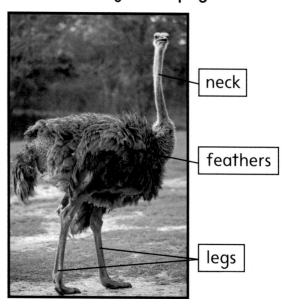

neck

feathers

legs